Ballroom Dances

FOR ALL

by Thomas E. Parson

Foreword

To many into whose hands it will fall, this book will be the only means of obtaining a working knowledge of the simple fundamentals necessary in becoming proficient in the social dances. To others who already dance it may prove a source of different step patterns with which to augment those already in use. In either case it is hoped the author's efforts will make easier and shorter the road to even more enjoyable participation in the most popular pastime in the world.

In everyone there is a natural impulse to move about in response to the rhythmic patterns of music. Some are *natural* dancers; in others the skill needed to lead or follow a partner must be *acquired* through training. Many in this latter category find the answer to their problems in dance groups that are supervised by qualified dance instructors, groups that provide the necessary instruction in the social dances together with the opportunity to practice with a variety of partners.

The author claims no personal credit for the invention or origin of any of the dances or of component parts of dances herein described; rather, he is deeply indebted to professional colleagues, and in particular the members of the Dance Educators of America, Inc., for the mutual exchange of ideas over a long period of years.

The Author.

O F the physical advantages of dancing there is in our minds not a single doubt. The total abandon to pleasure, the exhilaration of mind, and the exhuberance of spirits which characterize the members of our social dance groups are active agents in promoting health of body and cheerfulness of disposition.

But not for physical advantages alone do we of the Young Men's Christian Association commend dancing, for here is provided also a medium for bringing into pleasant social relation all ages of sexes; for destroying that feeling of diffidence and for correcting that shyness of manner which is best overcome by actual contact through an activity that provides the opportunity to meet, get acquainted, see, and be seen.

And when the combined physical and social advantages of dancing are summed up, the result is a recreational exercise for both the mind and the body. Certainly the cares and fatigue of the business and work day are no match for the stimulating force of the music, the temporary concentration on a new step shown by the group leader, the pleasure of renewed acquaintances and the making of new ones, the satisfaction of added skill in the Rumba, Tango, Lindy, Fox-Trot.

Contents

EXPLANATION OF TERMS AND ABBREVIATIONS

These terms and abbreviations compose the standard terminology used by dance teachers throughout the country. They eliminate the need for lengthy word pictures in the lessons which follow.

Arch............Place ball of free foot at instep of supporting foot with knee slightly flexed. No weight.

Balance.........Step on designated foot in direction indicated; sustain weight on that foot while free foot is used to Point, Arch, or Draw.

B-Ch...........Ball-Change. A combination of Press and Step in Place.

Bwd...........Backward.

Close..........Place free foot along side of supporting foot. Change weight.

Cortez (*Tango*)...Same as Dip, except that free foot remains in contact with floor.

Ch-Pos.........Challenge Position. Similar to OB-Pos, but man does not hold lady's hand.

C-Pos..........Closed Position. Also called "Waltz Position." Partners directly face each other or look over each other's right shoulder. Man hold's lady's right hand in his left hand; his right hand at her waist line; her left hand resting lightly on his right shoulder.

Dip (*Fox-Trot....*Step on designated foot in direction indi-
or *Waltz*)   cated; bend knee slightly to create swaying motion. Free foot is extended in opposite direction and may be off floor.

Draw..........Same as Close, except that weight is not transferred. The next step will always be on the designated foot.

Fwd...........Foward.

L..............Left foot.

1

LOD............Line of Direction (or Dance).

Lt..............Left.

OB-Pos........Open Break Position. Partners face each other and man holds lady's right hand in his left hand.

O-Pos..........Open (or Conversational) Position. Man and lady are side-by-side, facing in same direction. She stands at man's right side, with her left hand resting on his right shoulder. His right hand is at her waist line. Other hands not joined.

Point..........Extend free leg to direction indicated, with sole of foot raised so that only the tips of toes touch floor. No weight.

Press..........Exert just enough pressure on ball of foot to allow other foot to be raised and lowered in place.

Q..............Quick Step—weight sustained for one beat.

R..............Right foot.

Rt..............Right.

S..............Slow Step—weight sustained for two beats.

SIP............Step in Place. Raise and lower foot indicated without changing its position.

Swd...........Sideward.

Swd-close L-R...Step sideward on left foot; close right foot. Two changes of weight.

Swd-close R-L...Step sideward on right foot; close left foot. Two changes of weight.

Touch.........Extend foot to position indicated (fwd, swd, bwd); touch floor lightly with toe or heel. Foot remains free of weight and is used for succeeding step.

X L...........Cross left foot in back or in front (as indicated) of other foot; also "Press" may be indicated.

X R...........Cross right foot as above.

Dance Fundamentals

POSTURE AND BALANCE

THE phrase "if you can walk you can dance" is too often taken in too literal a sense. As a result, keen disappointment is experienced when it is discovered that the manner in which walking is practiced by some does not even slightly resemble dancing in its most elementary form. It may be correctly assumed, however, that a close relation between the two does exist; i.e., the feet are progressively moved from one point on the floor to another. It is, then, a natural conclusion that a person who can walk will be able to learn to dance.

Many of the common faults in walking reflect in a person's dancing. One of these is poor posture, the resultant effect of improper distribution of weight together with the manner in which the weight is transferred from one foot to another.

The first step in correcting faulty posture is to learn how to "take a load off the feet." Try it. Place the feet flat on the floor—*heels and toes together*. From the knees, stretch upward to bring the top of the head at least two inches nearer the ceiling. This action should pull in the lower abdomen and raise the diaphragm without stiffening or arching the shoulders. The head rests naturally, with chin up and forward—not pulled in against the chest. Raise the arms so that the upper arm is horizontal, the forearm vertical with palms forward.

Be sure to keep the feet flat on the floor during the process of relieving them of some of the usual but unnecessary strain.

3

THE PROGRESSIVE

Forward Movement

Now start walking slowly forward. Place the left foot —*heel down first*—on a direct line in front of the right foot. Do not permit the body to sag as the weight is transferred. Now place the right foot—*heel down first*—on a direct line in front of the left foot. Keep the weight up! Keep on walking, very slowly, with weight up and chin out. Soon a swinging motion from the hips downward will be noticed. Remember, though, to walk—save the dancing for later. Remember, too, that each foot is placed directly in front of the other.

The object of this exercise is an unbroken flow of motion as the weight is shifted from one foot to the other. Practice this phase diligently.

Now the actual dance movement can be started. The *ball* of foot, instead of heel, is first to make contact with the floor. No other change is made in stance or stride! As before, each foot is placed directly in front of the other —this time with ball of foot down first. As the weight is received, push the foot forward just a few inches before a complete transfer is made. *Do not rise on toes.* Practice this phase diligently.

Backward Movement

Start with the right foot and walk slowly backward. Place the right foot on a direct line in back of the left. The inside of the big toe is first to feel the weight, which is then released to the ball of the foot. Now place the left foot on a direct line in back of the right, and so on, very slowly. Keep the chin up!

Keep the knees *straight but not stiff* as the weight is shifted. Do not permit the body to sag as weight is transferred. Practice with arms in same position as described for the forward movement.

Jointly referred to as the "progressive," the forward and backward movements will develop poise, balance, and graceful carriage (posture)—the essentials to *improved* walking or dancing. It is necessary, then, that the progressive movements be practiced at every opportunity.

THE SIDEWARD-CLOSE MOVEMENT

The progressive movements having been developed to a point where the weight is carried upward to prevent slouching, the "sideward-close" is easily accomplished. Try it. Stand with heels and toes together. Raise the left heel, extend the left foot about twelve inches to the left side, on a line parallel with the right foot, and shift the weight to the left; now draw the right foot against the left and shift the weight to the right. Do this several times; then start with the right foot and do the sideward-close to the right.

Note particularly that the sideward-close is made up of two changes of weight—on the *sideward* movement and on the *closing* movement. Always remember this when combining the progressive and the sideward-close to create combinations for the Fox-Trot and other ballroom dances.

COMBINING THE PROGRESSIVE AND SIDEWARD-CLOSE

Taken singly, the progressive and the sideward-close become with practice simple operations; an attempt at combining the two can, however, create problems to be solved only by a thorough understanding of the basic principles of each, together with the close relation of one to the other.

For example, you have found in practice that the progressive movement is accomplished by placing one foot directly in front (or in back) of the other, by transferring the weight to that foot, and by following immediately with the other foot in the same direction. You have found, too, that the sideward-close is the result of moving one foot sideward (parallel with the other), transferring the weight to that foot, and immediately drawing the other alongside the first *with another transfer of weight!*

A combination well suited for practice, and containing all the elements of the foregoing, follows:

a) Stand with heels and toes together, arms raised;

b) start with left foot, take three steps forward on left, right, left, and end with weight on left;

c) with a continuous motion, draw the right foot forward until the ball of right is at side of and touching the heel of left, then move sideward on and transfer weight to right foot;

d) close left against right and shift weight to left;

e) start with right foot, take three backward steps on right, left, right, and end with weight on right;

f) with a continuous motion, draw the left foot backward until the heel of left is at side of and touching the fore part of right, then move sideward on and transfer weight to left foot;

g) close right against left and shift weight to right. *Start with left foot and repeat over and over.*

Abbreviated, this combination would be described as:

Fwd L-R-L—swd-close R-L
Bwd R-L-R—swd-close L-R.

SELF-ANALYZATION AND CORRECTION

Most of the difficulties encountered in effecting a combination of the progressive and sideward-close can be attributed (1) to a misunderstanding of the principles involving each, or (2) to a lack of ability heightened by failure to practice the application of these principles. In either case, there may be developed any of these three common faults:

1. Failure to move on a direct line forward (or backward), thus causing the feet to spread.

2. Failure to commence the sideward-close with a definite sideward movement, thus creating in many instances a duplication of the incorrect movement in fault 1.

3. Failure to shift the weight to the foot making the closing step in the sideward-close, which causes a start on the wrong foot.

These are but minor difficulties, to be overcome through a review and *closer* application of the basic principles of the progressive and sideward-close.

APPLICATION OF TIMING EFFECT

In some people there exists a natural inclination to respond with perfect timing to music played in any rhythm or tempo; in others the ability to keep time must be developed.

Dance music is played in even cadence, with a steady recurrence of certain beats to guide the dancer in both speed of movement and in determining the type of music being played—i.e., Waltz, Fox-Trot, Tango, Samba, etc.

The foregoing combination of the progressive and sideward-close is easily adapted to music played in 4/4, or Fox-Trot, time. Before proceeding, however, there must be established the difference between the meaning of (1) the musical count and (2) the dance count.

The *musical* count would represent the number and sequence of beats to the measure; for instance, 4/4 time denotes four beats (or musical counts) to the measure. Since a transfer of weight (or step) is not intended for each successive beat in Fox-Trot music, the *dance* count would denote the sequence of steps and whether the weight should be sustained on each succeeding transfer for two beats or for one, with these resultant expressions being used:

> *Slow Step* (S): on which the weight is sustained for two beats, and
>
> *Quick Step* (Q): on which the weight is sustained for one beat.

The application of Fox-Trot timing to the now familiar combination of progressive and sideward-close should provide a basis on which can be developed a sound working knowledge of the essentials necessary to become a good dancer.

MEAS-URE	MUSICAL COUNT	DANCE COUNT	DANCE MOVEMENT	TIME
1	1–2	1	Forward Left........	S
	3–4	2	Forward Right.......	S
2	1–2	3	Forward Left........	S
	3	4	Sideward Right......	Q
	4	and	Close Left to Right...	Q
3	1–2	5	Backward Right.....	S
	3–4	6	Backward Left.......	S
4	1–2	7	Backward Right.....	S
	3	8	Sideward Left........	Q
	4	and	Close Right to Left...	Q

Repeat over and over from 1st count.

THE SIMPLE TURNS

In establishing the basic approach to the simple turns, a single progressive combined with a sideward-close, reversed and repeated, is used. With their respective timing effects applied, this approach is standard for the Fox-Trot, Waltz, Tango, Samba, and Rumba.

It is advisable to develop the "feel" of the turning sequences before making an attempt at turning. For the left turn the sequence would be:

Fwd L—Swd-close R-L
Bwd R—Swd-close L-R

For the right turn the sequence is:

Fwd R—Swd-close L-R
Bwd L—Swd-close R-L

Once the feel of the approach to the turns has been developed, it is a simple matter to extend the movements into the desired turns. The accompanying diagrams show the approximate positions of the feet, together with the timing effect for the Fox-Trot. Note that perfect quarter-turns can be made on each turning sequence. The four walls of the room can be used as a guide in gauging the depth of the turns.

Left Turn (Fox-Trot Timing)   **Figure 1**

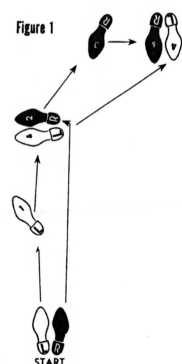

COUNT	TIME
1 Fwd L, turn to face center	S
2-& Swd-close R-L . . .	Q-Q
3 Bwd R, turn to face opposite LOD	S
4-& Swd-close L-R . . .	Q-Q

Repeat to end facing LOD.

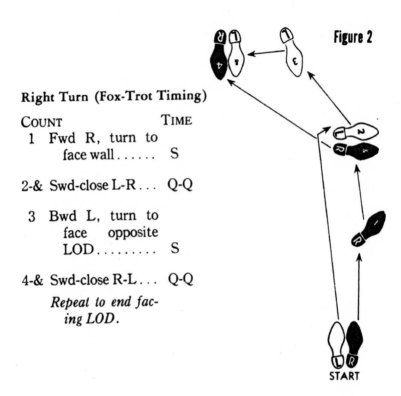

Figure 2

Right Turn (Fox-Trot Timing)

COUNT	TIME
1 Fwd R, turn to face wall......	S
2-& Swd-close L-R...	Q-Q
3 Bwd L, turn to face opposite LOD........	S
4-& Swd-close R-L...	Q-Q

Repeat to end facing LOD.

START

When practicing the turns with a partner, **the lady** moves *backward* on the R as the gentleman moves *forward* on the L, and vice versa.

LEADING AND FOLLOWING

In the process of mastering the simple basic technique there is developed in the dancer a co-ordination of movement that will eventually result in immediate response by all parts of the body to the impulses set up at the beginning of a step.

The man's lead would be described as "weak" if his body or his right arm should respond slowly to a forward, or to a turning, movement of the foot. And if his partner should continue with another backward step when he attempts a sideward-close he might again be blamed; but this might indicate, on the other hand, that the lady does not respond with sufficient ease to his lead.

It is obvious, then, that efficiency in both leading and following is to be measured in accordance with the individual's ability to consistently apply the aforementioned principles. It is also obvious that to effect a "strong" lead on his partner the man need not grasp her around the waist with a wrestler's hold.

A comfortable position having been taken by both partners, one in which both can move freely, the force necessary to propel the man's feet into predetermined positions will set up reactions throughout the body that will impel his partner to do the counterpart of his movement—*provided she is moving properly.*

The outward elements of leading and following can be summed up briefly. Both partners assume natural, comfortable positions. The man's elbows should be raised away from the body to an angle of at least forty-five degrees, or to a horizontal position. His right hand is placed at an advantageous spot between the lady's shoulders and waistline.

The lady's left arm should follow the line of the man's right arm, her left hand resting lightly on his right shoulder. *She must at all times carry her own weight.*

Both should retain a position in which each may look over the other's right shoulder. His left and her right hand may or may not be clasped, according to the style of dancing adopted at various times.

But above everything else—and to the exclusion of one or more of these generally-accepted rules—a natural attitude based on the principles already stressed should be assumed by both partners. Ballroom dancing is meant to be thoroughly enjoyed, and the pleasure derived from dancing with one partner as compared with another depends largely on the individual's knack of making his or her dancing conform to the laws of natural movement.

LINE OF DIRECTION

The counterclockwise course maintained in making progress around the dance floor is referred to as "Line of Direction" or "Line of Dance" (LOD).

When moving forward to LOD, the center of the room is at the man's left, the wall at his right; the lady, in moving backward to LOD, would have the center of the room at her right, the wall at her left.

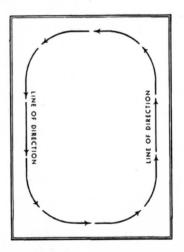

The necessity of adhering to the traffic rules of the dance floor should be obvious: it prevents unnecessary collisions and the confusion that would result if dancers were permitted to make progress in all directions.

The Fox-Trot

ONCE the dancer is able to define with precise movement the difference between the progressive and the sideward-close, the arrangement of varied combinations suitable for the Fox-Trot becomes a matter of fixing in one's mind a pattern consisting of a predetermined number of progressive steps to be followed with a sideward-close. Such arrangements may contain dips, pivots, left and right turns, cross steps, etc. These are all derivations of the basic progressive and sideward-close movements.

The combinations described on the pages immediately following are but a few of the many that are applicable to music played in 4/4 time. Once the knack of applying the basic principles outlined in the foregoing has been achieved, other combinations will suggest themselves.

Figure 4

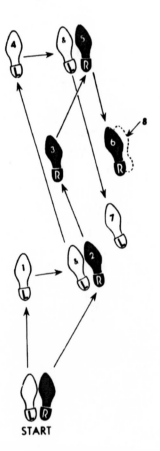

FIRST COMBINATION

Man's Part

COUNT		TIME
1	Fwd L..........	S
2-&	Swd-close R-L...	Q-Q
3	Fwd R.........	S
4	Fwd L..........	S
5-&	Swd-close R-L...	Q-Q
6	Bwd R.........	S
7	Dip bwd L......	S
8	Fwd R.........	S

Repeat from 1st count.

Figure 5

FIRST COMBINATION

Lady's Part

COUNT		TIME
1	Bwd R.........	S
2-&	Swd-close L-R...	Q-Q
3	Bwd L.........	S
4	Bwd R........	S
5-&	Swd-close L-R...	Q-Q
6	Fwd L.........	S
7	Dip fwd R......	S
8	Bwd L.........	S

Repeat from 1st count.

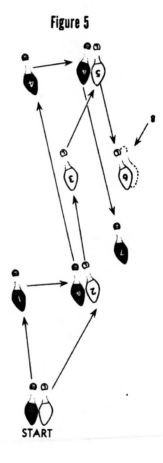

START

Figure 6

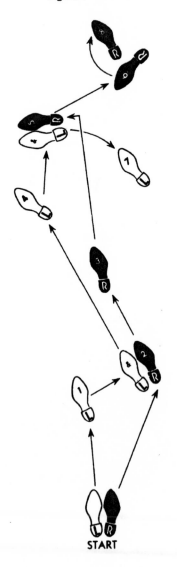

SECOND COMBINATION

Man's Part

COUNT		TIME
1	Fwd L..........	S
2-&	Swd-close R-L...	Q-Q
3	Fwd R.........	S
4	Fwd L, turn to face center....	S
5-&	Swd-close R-L...	Q-Q
6	Bwd R.........	S
7	Dip bwd L, turn to LOD.......	S
8	Fwd R to face LOD.........	S

Repeat from 1st count or combine with previous combination.

Figure 7

SECOND COMBINATION

Lady's Part

COUNT		TIME
1	Bwd R.........	S
2-&	Swd-close L-R...	Q-Q
3	Bwd L..........	S
4	Bwd R, turn to face wall......	S
5-&	Swd-close L-R...	Q-Q
6	Fwd L..........	S
7	Dip fwd R, turn to face opposite LOD.........	S
8	Bwd L to LOD...	S

Repeat from 1st count or combine with previous combination.

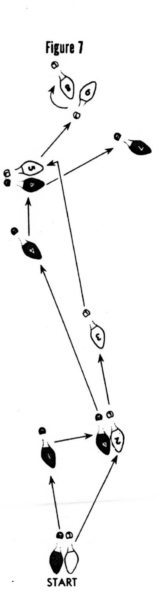

START

Figure 8

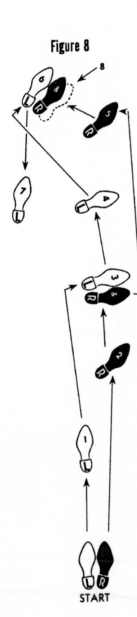

THIRD COMBINATION

Man's Part

COUNT		TIME
1	Fwd L..........	S
2	Fwd R, turn to face wall......	S
3-&	Swd-close L-R...	Q-Q
4	Swd L, to LOD..	S
5	Cross R between self and partner	S
6-&	Swd-close L-R, turn to LOD...	Q-Q
7	Dip bwd L......	S
8	Fwd R to face LOD.........	S

Repeat from 1st count.

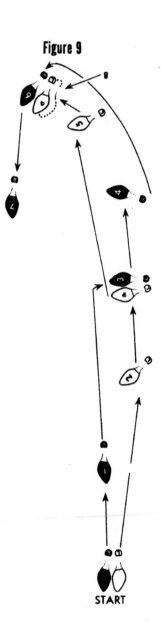

Figure 9

THIRD COMBINATION

Lady's Part

COUNT		TIME
1	Bwd R.........	S
2	Bwd L, turn to face center....	S
3-&	Swd-close R-L...	Q-Q
4	Swd R, to LOD..	S
5	Cross L between self and partner	S
6-&	Swd-close R-L, turn to opposite LOD.........	Q-Q
7	Dip fwd R.......	S
8	Bwd L to face opposite LOD....	S

Repeat from 1st count.

START

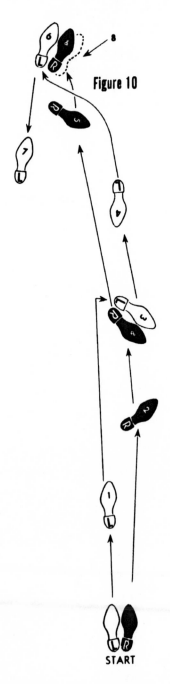

Figure 10

FOURTH COMBINATION

Man's Part

COUNT		TIME
1	Fwd L..........	S
2	Fwd R, turn to face wall......	S
3-&	Swd-close L-R, end facing opposite LOD....	Q-Q
4	Bwd L, opposite LOD.........	S
5	Bwd R, turn to face wall......	S
6-&	Swd-close L-R, end facing LOD	Q-Q
7	Dip bwd L......	S
8	Fwd R..........	S

Repeat from 1st count.

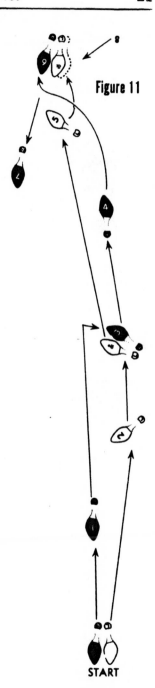

Figure 11

FOURTH COMBINATION

Lady's Part

COUNT		TIME
1	Bwd R.........	S
2	Bwd L, turn to face center....	S
3-&	Swd-close R-L, end facing LOD	Q-Q
4	Fwd R, to LOD..	S
5	Fwd L, turn to face center....	S
6-&	Swd-close R-L, end facing opposite LOD....	Q-Q
7	Dip fwd R.......	S
8	Bwd L..........	S

Repeat from 1st count.

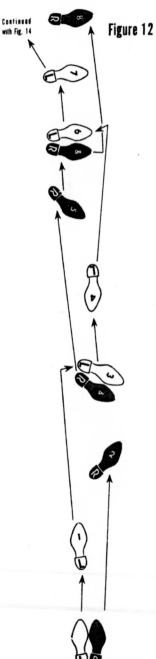

Continued with Fig. 14

Figure 12

FIFTH COMBINATION

Man's Part

COUNT		TIME
1	Fwd L..........	S
2	Fwd R, turn to face wall......	S
3-&	Swd-close L-R, end facing opposite LOD...	Q-Q
4	Bwd L to LOD...	S
5	Bwd R, turn to face wall......	S
6-&	Swd-close L-R, end facing wall.	Q-Q
7	Swd L, to LOD..	S
8	Cross R between self and partner	S

Continue with 6th combination.

START

Figure 13

FIFTH COMBINATION

Lady's Part

COUNT		TIME
1	Bwd R..........	S
2	Bwd L, turn to face center	S
3-&	Swd-close R-L, end facing LOD	Q-Q
4	Fwd R to LOD ..	S
5	Fwd L, turn to face center	S
6-&	Swd-close R-L, end facing center	Q-Q
7	Swd R to LOD...	S
8	Cross L between self and partner	S

Continue with 6th combination.

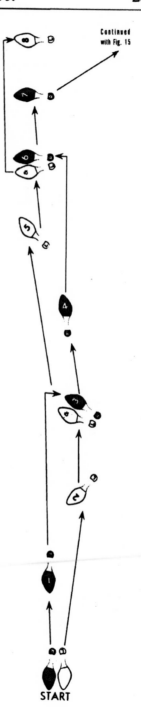

Continued with Fig. 15

START

Figure 14

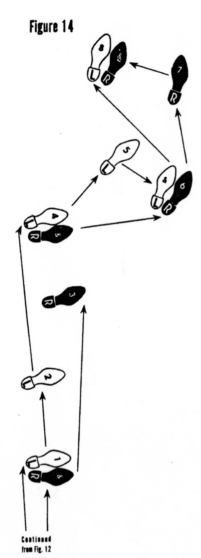

Continued
from Fig. 12

SIXTH COMBINATION

Man's Part

COUNT		TIME
	Start facing wall:	
1-&	Swd-close L-R to LOD.......	Q-Q
2	Swd L..........	S
3	Cross R between self and partner	S
4-&	Swd-close L-R...	Q-Q
5	Fwd L to wall....	S
6-&	Swd-close R-L...	Q-Q
7	Cross R between self and partner	S
8-&	Swd-close L-R, end facing LOD	Q-Q

Repeat from 1st count of previous combination.

Figure 15

SIXTH COMBINATION

Lady's Part

COUNT		TIME

Start facing center:

1-& Swd-close   R-L
      to LOD . . . . Q-Q

2   Swd R . . . . S

3   Cross L between
     self and partner S

4-& Swd-close R-L . . . Q-Q

5   Bwd R to wall . . . S

6-& Swd-close L-R . . . Q-Q

7   Cross L between
     self and partner S

8-& Swd-close   R-L,
     end facing op-
     posite LOD . . . . Q-Q

*Repeat from 1st count of
previous combination.*

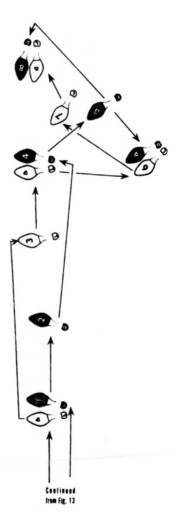

Continued
from Fig. 13

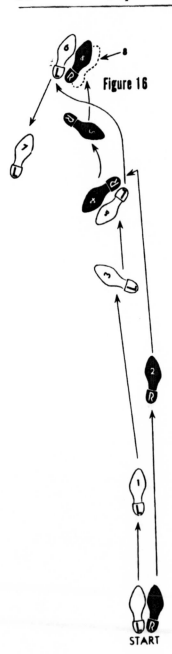

Figure 16

SEVENTH COMBINATION

Man's Part

COUNT		TIME
1	Fwd L..........	S
2	Fwd R..........	S
3	Fwd L, turn to face center....	*S
4-&	Swd-close R-L, end facing opposite LOD....	*Q-Q
5	Bwd R, turn to face wall......	*S
6-&	Swd-close L-R, end facing LOD	*Q-Q
7	Dip bwd L......	S
8	Fwd R..........	S

Repeat from 1st count.
*This is a complete left turn.

START

SEVENTH COMBINATION Figure 17

Lady's Part

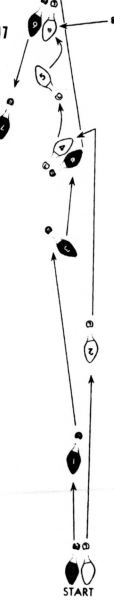

Count		Time
1	Bwd R.........	S
2	Bwd L..........	S
3	Bwd R, turn to face wall......	*S
4-&	Swd-close L-R, end facing LOD	*Q-Q
5	Fwd L, turn to face center....	*S
6-&	Swd-close R-L, end facing opposite LOD....	*Q-Q
7	Dip fwd R.......	S
8	Bwd L.........	S

Repeat from 1st count.
**This is a complete left turn.*

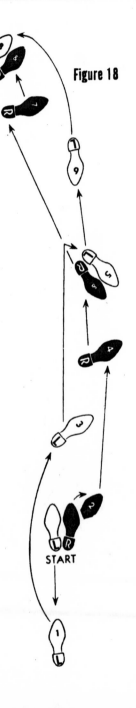

Figure 18

EIGHTH COMBINATION

Man's Part

COUNT		TIME
1	Dip bwd L	S
2	Fwd R, turn to face wall	S
3	Swd L to LOD . . .	S
4	Cross R between self and partner	S
5-&	Swd-close L-R, turn Rt to end facing opposite LOD	Q-Q
6	Bwd L to LOD . . .	S
7	Bwd R, turn Lt to face wall	S
8-&	Swd-close L-R, turn Lt to end facing LOD	Q-Q

Repeat from 1st count.

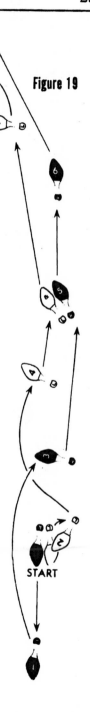

Figure 19

EIGHTH COMBINATION

Lady's Part

COUNT		TIME
1	Dip fwd R.......	S
2	Bwd L, turn to face center....	S
3	Swd R to LOD...	S
4	Cross L between self and partner	S
5-&	Swd-close R-L, turn Rt to end facing LOD....	Q-Q
6	Fwd R to LOD...	S
7	Fwd L, turn Lt to face center....	S
8-&	Swd-close R-L, turn Lt to end facing opposite LOD.........	Q-Q

Repeat from 1st count.

NINTH COMBINATION

Man's Part

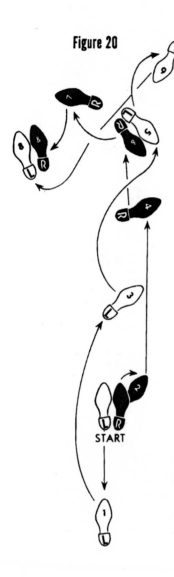

Figure 20

COUNT		TIME
1	Dip bwd L......	S
2	Fwd R, turn Rt to face wall......	*S
3	Swd L to LOD...	*S
4	Cross R between self and partner	*S
5-&	Swd-close L-R, turn Rt to end facing opposite LOD.........	*Q-Q
6	Dip bwd L, pivot Rt to face center..........	*S
7	Fwd R, turn Rt to face LOD...	*S
8-&	Swd-close L-R, end facing LOD	Q-Q

Repeat from 1st count.
*This is a complete right turn.

START

NINTH COMBINATION

Lady's Part

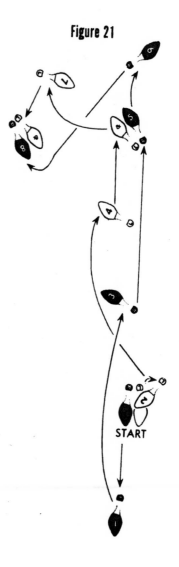

Figure 21

COUNT		TIME
1	Dip fwd R.......	S
2	Bwd L, turn Rt to face center....	*S
3	Swd R to LOD...	*S
4	Cross L between self and partner	*S
5-&	Swd-close R-L, turn Rt to end facing LOD....	*Q-Q
6	Dip fwd R, pivot Rt to end facing wall..........	*S
7	Bwd L, turn Rt to face opposite LOD........	*S
8-&	Swd-close R-L, turn Rt to end facing opposite LOD........	Q-Q

Repeat from 1st count.
**This is a complete right turn.*

The Waltz

W RITTEN in 3/4 time (three beats to the measure)
Waltz music is interpreted basically with a change
of weight from one foot to the other on each successive beat of the music, with added emphasis on the
step corresponding to the first beat in each measure.
The weight is sustained on each transfer for an *equal length
of time* except when the "hesitation" is applied. As a
consequence, the steps of the Waltz are not referred to as
slow and *quick* in the application of timing effect.

An unalterable rule in Waltzing concerns the "closing"
step: it is always made on the third beat of a measure—
never on a first or second beat. This does not mean that a
closing step must be made on each successive third beat;
it means only that when used in a combination the closing
step occurs on a third beat.

The expression "Swd-close" being so closely identified with two *quick* steps (4/4 time), the same movement in Waltz (3/4 time) is described as two individual steps: i.e., *swd L. (or R)* and *close R (or L)*.

Except in some forms of hesitation, the first beat of the measure is represented by a forward (or backward) step on which more emphasis is placed than on the two succeeding (swd-close) steps. When applied to the basic approach to the simple Waltz turns, the resultant timing effect is:

DANCE MOVEMENT

MEAS-URE	MUSIC COUNT	LEFT TURN	RIGHT TURN	DANCE COUNT
1	1	Fwd L	Fwd R	1
	2	Swd R	Swd L	2
	3	Close L	Close R	3
2	1	Bwd R	Bwd L	4
	2	Swd L	Swd R	5
	3	Close R	Close L	6

The diagrams on Pages 9-10 show the approximate foot positions for the Waltz turns. Care should be exercised, however, in applying the proper timing and in distinguishing the difference between the effects of Fox-Trot and Waltz timing when applied to the same sequence of movement.

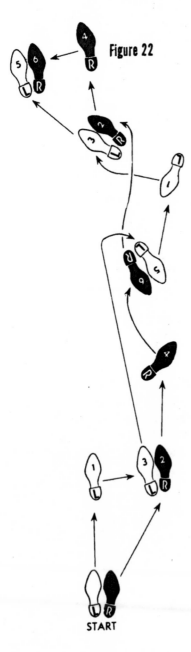

Figure 22

FIRST COMBINATION

Man's Part—The Right Turn

COUNT

1 Fwd L

2 Swd R

3 Close L

4 Fwd R ⎫ *Turn Rt. to*
          ⎪ *face   wall,*
5 Swd L ⎬ *end facing*
          ⎪ *opposite*
6 Close R ⎭ *LOD.*

1 Bwd L ⎫
          ⎪
2 Swd R ⎪ *Turn Rt. to*
          ⎪ *face center,*
3 Close L ⎬ *end facing*
          ⎪ *LOD.*
4 Fwd R ⎪

5 Swd L ⎭

6 Close R

FIRST COMBINATION

Lady's Part—The Right Turn

COUNT

1 Bwd R

2 Swd L

3 Close R

4 Bwd L ⎫ *Turn Rt. to*
          ⎬ *face center,*
5 Swd R ⎪ *end facing*
          ⎪ *LOD.*
6 Close L ⎭

1 Fwd R   ⎫
           ⎪
2 Swd L   ⎪ *Turn Rt. to*
           ⎬ *face wall,*
3 Close R ⎪ *end facing*
           ⎪ *opposite*
4 Bwd L   ⎪ *LOD.*
           ⎭
5 Swd R

6 Close L

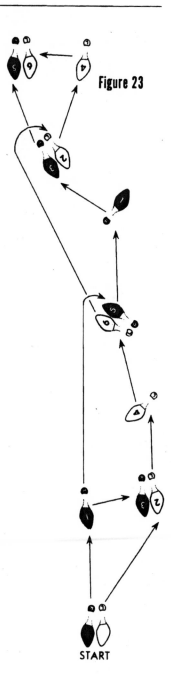

Figure 23

START

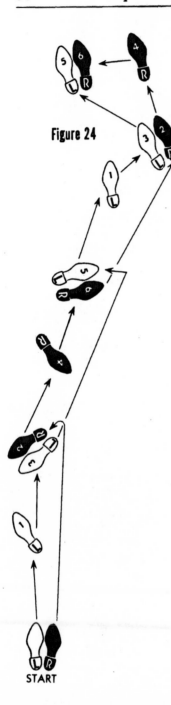

Figure 24

SECOND COMBINATION

Man's Part—The Left Turn

COUNT

1	Fwd L	
2	Swd R	*Turn Lt. to face center,*
3	Close L	*end facing opposite LOD.*
4	Bwd R	
5	Swd L	*Turn Lt. to face wall.*
6	Close R	

1	Fwd L	
2	Swd R	*Turn Lt. to end facing LOD.*
3	Close L	
4	Fwd R	
5	Swd L	
6	Close R	

START

SECOND COMBINATION

Lady's Part—The Left Turn

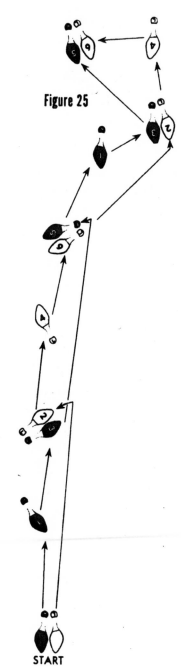

Figure 25

COUNT

1	Bwd R	*Turn Lt. to face wall, end facing LOD.*
2	Swd L	
3	Close R	

4	Fwd L	*Turn Lt. to face center.*
5	Swd R	
6	Close L	

1	Bwd R	*Turn Lt. to end facing opposite LOD.*
2	Swd L	
3	Close R	

4 Bwd L

5 Swd R

6 Close L

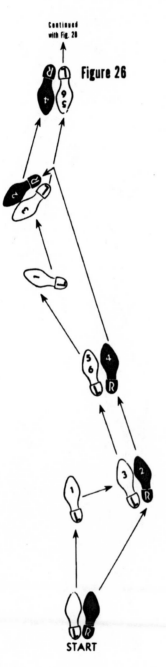

Continued with Fig. 28

Figure 26

THIRD COMBINATION

Man's Part—The Hesitation

COUNT

1 Fwd L

2 Swd R

3 Close L

4 Fwd R

5–6 Draw L to R, no weight on L

1 Fwd L ⎫ *Turn Lt. to face center, end facing opposite LOD.*
2 Swd R ⎬
3 Close L ⎭

4 Bwd R to LOD

5–6 Draw L to R, no weight on L

Continue with 4th combination.

START

THIRD COMBINATION

Lady's Part—The Hesitation

COUNT

1 Bwd R

2 Swd L

3 Close R

4 Bwd L

5–6 Draw R to L, no
weight on R

1 Bwd R ⎫
           ⎪ *Turn Lt. to*
2 Swd L ⎬ *face wall,*
           ⎪ *end facing*
3 Close R ⎭ *LOD.*

4 Fwd L to LOD

5–6 Draw R to L, no
weight on R

*Continue with 4th com-
bination.*

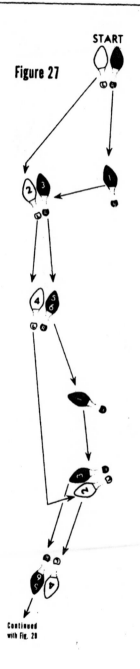

Figure 27

START

Continued
with Fig. 28

FOURTH COMBINATION

Figure 28

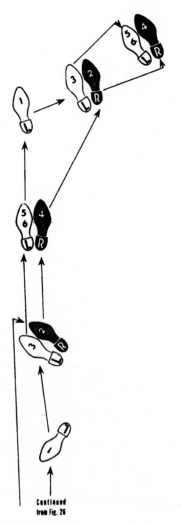

Continued
from Fig. 26

Man's Part—The Hesitation

COUNT

Start facing opposite LOD:

1   Bwd L ⎫ *Turn Rt. to*
           ⎪ *face center*
2   Swd R ⎬ *end facing*
           ⎪ *LOD.*
3   Close L ⎭

4   Fwd R to LOD

5–6 Draw L to R, no weight on L

1   Fwd L

2   Swd R

3   Close L

4   Swd R to wall

5–6 Draw L to R, no weight on L

Repeat from beginning of 3rd combination.

FOURTH COMBINATION

Lady's Part—The Hesitation   **Figure 29**

<small>Count</small>

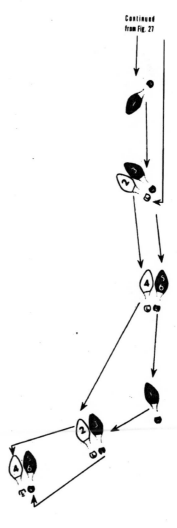

Start facing LOD:

	Fwd R	*Turn Rt. to face wall, end facing opposite LOD.*
2	Swd L	
3	Close R	

4   Bwd L to LOD

5–6   Draw R to L, no weight on R

1   Bwd R

2   Swd L

3   Close R

4   Swd L to wall

5–6   Draw R to L, no weight on R

Repeat from beginning of 3rd combination.

Continued from Fig. 27

FIFTH COMBINATION

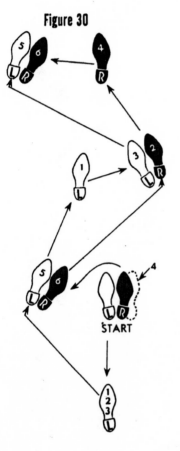

Figure 30

Man's Part

Count

1-2-3 Dip bwd L

   4 Fwd R

   5 Swd L

   6 Close R

   1 Fwd L

   2 Swd R

   3 Close L

   4 Cross R between self and partner

   5 Swd L

   6 Close R

FIFTH COMBINATION

Lady's Part

COUNT

1-2-3 Dip Fwd R

4 Bwd L

5 Swd R

6 Close L

1 Bwd R

2 Swd L

3 Close R

4 Cross L between self
   and partner

5 Swd R

6 Close L

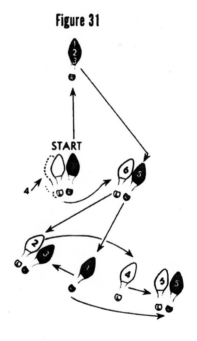

Figure 31

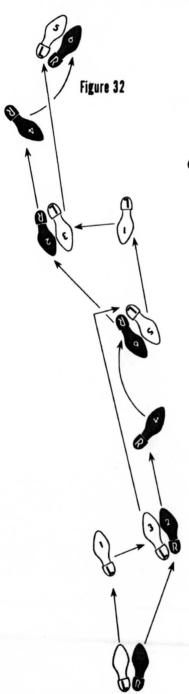

Figure 32

SIXTH COMBINATION

Man's Part

COUNT

Count	Step	
1	Fwd L	
2	Swd R	
3	Close L	
4	Fwd R	*Turn Rt. to face wall, end facing opposite LOD.*
5	Swd L	
6	Close R	
1	Bwd L	
2	Swd R	
3	Close L	
4	Bwd R	*Turn Lt. to face wall, end facing LOD.*
5	Swd L	
6	Close R	

SIXTH COMBINATION

Lady's Part

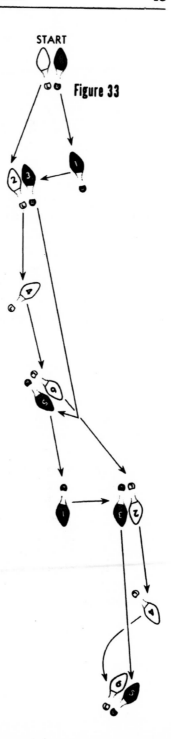

Figure 33

COUNT

1　Bwd R

2　Swd L

3　Close R

4　Bwd L ⎫
　　　　　⎬ *Turn Rt. to*
5　Swd R ⎨ *face center,*
　　　　　⎪ *end facing*
6　Close L ⎭ *LOD.*

1　Fwd R

2　Swd L

3　Close R

4　Fwd L ⎫ *Turn Lt. to*
　　　　　⎪ *face center,*
5　Swd R ⎬ *end facing*
　　　　　⎪ *opposite*
6　Close L ⎭ *LOD.*

The Rumba

THE Rumba's distinguishing feature is its style of execution. The steps are extremely simple, being based on an elementary combination of the sideward-close and progressive. The timing effect, also elementary, is a constant repetition of the familiar *quick-quick-slow . . . quick-quick-slow*.

It remains, then, for the dancer to concern himself mainly with mastering the intricacies of the Rumba's style, without which even a perfect application of timing effect to step pattern would resemble too closely the Fox-Trot.

The position assumed by partners differs from the other ballroom dances, and aids in effecting the style of movement. The feet of the partners are close together, while their bodies seldom make contact. The man holds the lady well away from him, with his right hand at her waist. Both lean slightly back from the hips, with the lady pressing backward against the man's right hand. Her left arm extends so that her hand rests lightly on his right shoulder.

The man's left hand and the lady's right hand are joined, with elbows raised away from sides, forearms vertical, palms forward. The knees are kept close together and completely relaxed; steps are extremely short, with the force of action downward from the knees. On each transfer of weight the feet are flat on the floor—do not dance on toes! Any movement of the torso is an involuntary reaction and the shoulders are not raised and lowered.

The forward and backward steps are longer, and taken with more emphasis than the side steps. A thorough understanding of the progressive and sideward-close will enable the dancer to grasp more readily the basic steps of the Rumba.

THE BASIC STEPS AND TIMING EFFECT

It should be particularly noted that the Rumba is commenced with a *sideward* movement on the first beat of the measure; also, that the pause or *slow* step is on the third and fourth beats. The basic patterns of the Rumba which are shown below should be practiced without trying to apply the turning movements until the correct timing effect has been achieved.

DANCE MOVEMENT

MEAS- URE	MUSIC COUNT	LEFT TURN	RIGHT TURN	DANCE COUNT	TIME
1	1	Swd L	Swd R	1	Q
	2	Close R	Close L	&	Q
	3–4	Fwd L	Fwd R	2	S
2	1	Swd R	Swd L	3	Q
	2	Close L	Close R	&	Q
	3–4	Bwd R	Bwd L	4	S

Repeat from 1st count.

If the sideward steps are short enough, and the forward and backward steps long enough, the above patterns will form a "box" that will be oblong in shape.

When immediate progression is needed, the dancer may substitute a *forward* step for the backward step on the fourth dance count.

FIRST COMBINATION

With Left Turn

	Man's Part	Lady's Part	
COUNT			TIME
1-&	Swd-close L-R	Swd-close R-L	Q-Q
2	Fwd L	Bwd R	S
3-&	Swd-close R-L	Swd-close L-R	Q-Q
4	Fwd R	Bwd L	S
5-&	Swd-close L-R	Swd-close R-L	Q-Q
6	Fwd L, turn Lt	Bwd R, turn Lt	S
7-&	Swd-close R-L	Swd-close L-R	Q-Q
8	Bwd R, turn Lt	Fwd L, turn Lt	S
1-&	Swd-close L-R	Swd-close R-L	Q-Q
2	Fwd L, turn Lt	Bwd R, turn Lt	S
3-&	Swd-close R-L	Swd-close L-R	Q-Q
4	Bwd R, turn Lt	Fwd L, turn Lt	S
5-&	Swd-close L-R	Swd-close R-L	Q-Q
6	Fwd L, turn Lt	Bwd R, turn Lt	S
7-&	Swd-close R-L	Swd-close L-R	Q-Q
8	Bwd R, turn Lt	Fwd L, turn Lt	S

The first 8 counts can be repeated as desired, with progress being made to LOD, by ignoring the directions to turn left on 6th and 8th counts. A complete left turn is intended on the second group of 8 counts.

Extreme care should be exercised when making the turn, to keep the feet close together, with a very short sideward movement to commence the sideward-close.

SECOND COMBINATION

	Man's Part	Lady's Part	
COUNT			TIME
1-&	Swd-close L-R	Swd-close R-L	Q-Q
2	Fwd L	Bwd R	S
3-&	Swd-close R-L	Swd-close L-R	Q-Q
4	Fwd R	Bwd L	S
5-&	Swd-close L-R	Swd-close R-L	Q-Q
6	Bwd L, turn Rt	Fwd R, turn Rt	S
7-&	Swd-close R-L	Swd-close L-R	Q-Q
8	Fwd R, turn Rt	Bwd L, turn Rt	S
1-&	Swd-close L-R	Swd-close R-L	Q-Q
2	Bwd L, turn Rt	Fwd R, turn Rt	S
3-&	Swd-close R-L	Swd-close L-R	Q-Q
4	Fwd R, turn Rt	Bwd L, turn Rt	S
5-&	Swd-close L-R	Swd-close R-L	Q-Q
6	Bwd L, turn Rt	Fwd R, turn R	S
7-&	Swd-close R-L	Swd-close L-R	Q-Q
8	Fwd R, turn Rt	Bwd L, turn Rt	S

Rumba turns should be made with a gradual, rather than a sharp turning movement. When done in this manner more time is used and more steps are required than in Fox-Trot and Waltz turns; hence the turns can be commenced on the 6th count of the first group in both the 1st and 2nd combinations.

THIRD COMBINATION

Count	Man's Part	Lady's Part	Time
1-&	Swd-close L-R	Swd-close R-L	Q-Q
2	Fwd L	Bwd R	S
3-&	Swd-close R-L	Swd-close L-R	Q-Q
4	Fwd R	Bwd L	S
5-&	Swd-close L-R	Swd-close R-L	Q-Q
6	Bwd L	Bwd R	S
7-&	Swd-close R-L	Swd-close L-R	Q-Q
8	Fwd R	Fwd L	S

Repeat as desired, or combine with:

Count	Man's Part	Lady's Part	Time
1-&	Swd-close L-R	Swd-close R-L	Q-Q
2	Fwd L	Bwd R	S
3-&	Swd-close R-L	Swd-close L-R	Q-Q
4	Bwd R	Bwd L	S
5-&	Swd-close L-R	Swd-close R-L	Q-Q
6	Fwd L	Fwd R	S
7-&	Swd-close R-L	Swd-close L-R	Q-Q
8	Fwd R	Bwd L	S

Note that on the 6th count of first group both partners step *backward*, drawing away from each other. The man's left and his partner's right hand remain clasped, while his right and her left hand become disengaged but with *arms held up*. On 8th count partners resume original position.

On the 4th count of the second group partners again draw away from each other with a backward step, resuming original position on 8th count.

FOURTH COMBINATION

	Man's Part	Lady's Part	
COUNT			TIME
1-&	Swd-close L-R	Swd-close R-L	Q-Q
2	Fwd L	Bwd R	S
3-&	Swd-close R-L	Swd-close L-R	Q-Q
4	Bwd R	Fwd L	S
5-&	Swd-close L-R	Swd-close R-L	Q-Q
6	Bwd L	Bwd R	S
7-&	Swd-close R-L	Swd-close L-R	Q-Q
8	SIP on R	Fwd L	S
1-&	SIP on L-R	Fwd R-L	Q-Q
2	SIP on L	Fwd R	S
3-&	SIP on R-L	Fwd L-R	Q-Q
4	SIP on R	Fwd L	S
5-&	SIP on L-R	Fwd R-L	Q-Q
6	SIP on L	Fwd R	S
7-&	Swd-close R-L	Swd-close L-R	Q-Q
8	Fwd R	Bwd L	S

Again the partners move away from each other on the 6th count, this time in preparation for the lady to circle the man, thus: from the 8th count of the first group through the 6th count of the second group the man's steps are taken "in place," while the lady performs a complete circle, moving *forward* to his right side and around the man to end in original position on the 7th count. As the man commences his *in place* movements he shifts her right hand to his right hand, and as she circles around him he reaches behind him and again takes her right in his left hand to guide her to original position.

FIFTH COMBINATION

Count	Man's Part	Lady's Part	Time
1-&	Swd-close L-R	Swd-close R-L	Q-Q
2	Fwd L	Bwd R	S
3-&	Swd-close R-L	Swd-close L-R	Q-Q
4	Swd R	Swd L	S
5	Press ball of L in back of R	Press ball of R in back of L	Q
&	SIP on R	SIP on L	Q
6	Swd L	Swd R	S
7	Press ball of R in back of L	Press ball of L in back of R	Q
&	SIP on L	SIP on R	Q
8	Swd R	Swd L	S
&	Strike L against R, no weight on L	Strike R against L, no weight on R	S

Repeat as desired from 1st count.

The movement created on counts 5-& and 7-& is a "ball-change": i.e., foot is swung into position indicated (L in back of R), and, with weight remaining forward and over R, ball of L is pressed to floor, releasing weight momentarily from R. The weight is instantly shifted to R without that foot having been moved from its place.

It is intended that an eventual sway of the body shall accompany the ball-change movements. The man, facing LOD, will develop a slight turn of the body to face the center of the room as he swings his L back of R for the "ball-"; on the "change," he will turn again to LOD. The lady, facing opposite LOD, will develop a slight turn to face the center when she commences the ball-change on her R. These directions are reversed when the ball-changes are commenced on the other foot of the man and the lady.

When the partners turn (simultaneously) to face the center on a ball-change, the man's left and the lady's right hand become disengaged, but remain elevated. On the turn to face the wall, the other hands leave their accustomed position, the man's at the lady's waist and the lady's on his shoulder, and these also are kept raised until their return to the original position.

The Samba

THE Samba is quite the liveliest of the ballroom dances introduced to the United States from Latin America. Its music possesses a rollicking rhythm which suggests a style of movement that can become as boisterous as any created by north-of-the-border jive!

A correct application of timing effect to step pattern is of the utmost importance, even more so in the beginning than the style of movement, for it will be found that the Samba's style is closely connected with the rhythmical reaction set up when correct timing has been achieved.

The basic step pattern consists of the same movements learned in the Fox-Trot and Waltz: *fwd-swd-close* . . . *bwd-swd-close*. The timing is different from either of these dances and must be closely adhered to in sequence: *quick-quick-slow* . . . *quick-quick-slow*.

THE BASIC STEP PATTERN AND TIMING EFFECT

DANCE MOVEMENT

MEAS-URE	MUSIC COUNT	LEFT TURN	RIGHT TURN	DANCE COUNT	TIME
1	1	Fwd L	Fwd R	1	Q
	2	Swd R	Swd L	&	Q
	3-4	Close L	Close R	2	S
2	1	Bwd R	Bwd L	3	Q
	2	Swd L	Swd R	&	Q
	3-4	Close R	Close L	4	S

Note particularly that it is on the *closing* step that the pause is effected—not on the forward and backward steps as in the Fox-Trot and Rumba. This is one of the distinguishing features of the Samba and must be strictly adhered to, else the result will resemble a mixture of the Fox-Trot and Rumba.

In performing the basic steps described above, partners may assume the position used in the Rumba. The rhythmical reaction which provides Samba style can best be explained as: DOWN-up-DOWN . ... DOWN-up-DOWN. On the forward step the movement of the body is accented *downward;* on the sideward step, *upward;* on the closing step, *downward.*

The sideward step is taken on the ball of the foot, and with the quick closing step a ball-change is effected, resulting in a movement described as: *step-ball-change* . . . *step-ball-change.* At times the "change" is not a closing step at all; rather, it becomes an accented movement of the foot "in place."

FIRST COMBINATION

	Man's Part	Lady's Part	TIME
COUNT			
1	Fwd L	Bwd R	Q
&-2	Swd-close R-L	Swd-close L-R	Q-S
3	Bwd R	Bwd L	Q
&-4	Swd-close L-R	Swd-close R-L	Q-S
5	Fwd L	Bwd R	Q
&-6	Swd-close R-L	Swd-close L-R	Q-Q
&-7	Swd-close R-L	Swd-close L-R	Q-Q
&-8	Swd-close R-L	Swd-close L-R	Q-S
1	Fwd R	Bwd L	Q
&-2	Swd-close L-R	Swd-close R-L	Q-S
3	Bwd L	Fwd R	Q
&-4	Swd-close R-L	Swd-close L-R	Q-S
5	Fwd R	Bwd L	Q
&-6	Swd-close L-R	Swd-close R-L	Q-Q
&-7	Swd-close L-R	Swd-close R-L	Q-Q
&-8	Swd-close L-R	Swd-close R-L	Q-S

Repeat as desired from 1st count.

Partners may assume the closed or the Rumba position when dancing the above combination.

SECOND COMBINATION

In this combination the ball-change is used to effect the "paddle-turn," with the sideward step serving as the paddle which helps to make complete left or right turns in four counts.

At the beginning the man lets go his hold on the lady, and each performs the paddle-turn individually, the man turning to his *left* as the lady turns to her *right*, and vice versa.

	Man's Part	Lady's Part	
COUNT			TIME
1	Fwd L, turn sharply *left* to face center	Fwd R, turn sharpiy *right* to face center	Q
&	Press ball of R swd	Press ball of L swd	Q
2	SIP on L, pivoting to face opposite LOD	SIP on R, pivoting to face LOD	Q
&	Press ball of R swd	Press ball of L swd	Q
3	SIP on L, pivoting to face wall	SIP on R, pivoting to face wall	Q
&	Press ball of R swd	Press ball of L swd	Q
4	SIP on L, pivoting to face LOD and partner	SIP on R, pivoting to face opposite LOD and partner	S
5	Fwd R, turn sharply *right* to face wall	Fwd L, turn sharply *left* to face wall	Q
&	Press ball of L swd	Press ball of R swd	Q
6	SIP on R, pivoting to face opposite LOD, back to partner	SIP on L, pivoting to face LOD, back to partner	Q
&	Press ball of L swd	Press ball of R swd	Q
7	SIP on R, pivoting to face center	SIP on L, pivoting to face center	Q
&	Press ball of L swd	Press ball of R swd	Q
8	SIP on R, pivoting to face LOD and partner	SIP on L, pivoting to face opposite LOD and partner	S

Repeat or combine with 1st combination.

Note that partners are back to back on 2nd and 6th counts.

THIRD COMBINATION

Here is a step pattern that will require a complete co-ordination of body movement in order to apply to it correctly the Samba's timing effect. Partners may assume either the conversational or the half-open position, as both move forward and backward simultaneously.

COUNT	Man's Part	Lady's Part	TIME
1	Short step fwd on L	Short step fwd on R	Q
&	Step bwd a few inches on ball of R	Step bwd a few inches on ball of L	Q
2	Pull L bwd toward R a few inches— do not close	Pull R bwd toward L a few inches— do not close	S
3	Short step fwd on R	Short step fwd on L	Q
&	Step bwd a few inches on ball of L	Step bwd a few inches on ball of R	Q
4	Pull R bwd toward L a few inches— do not close	Pull L bwd toward R a few inches— do not close	S

Repeat from 1st count.

Note particularly that at no time are the feet brought to the closed position; also, that the movement on counts 1-& and 3-& comprise a "rocking" movement foward and backward.

Combine the above with the paddle-turn described in the 2nd combination; with both partners facing LOD in the conversational or half-open position, the man will commence the paddle-turn by turning sharply on his L to face the center, while the lady will turn on her R to face the wall.

The Tango

TANGO music is written and played in both 2/4 and 4/4 time; in either, the dance is based on two *slow* steps to each measure of music, with extra (*quick*) steps taken between the beats (2/4) or on the second and fourth beats (4/4) to provide a basis for variation.

In the Tango, proficiency in the style of movement peculiar to this type of dance is just as important as step combinations. The music itself will suggest a basis for this style: a slow, somewhat languorous movement with a sharp definition of the progressive and the sideward and closing steps.

A preliminary study of the following combinations will reveal that a timing effect different from that of the Fox-Trot or the Waltz has been applied. Careful attention must be paid to this phase of the Tango, else the dancer will perform a series of movements that will too closely resemble those applied to Fox-Trot music.

Figure 34

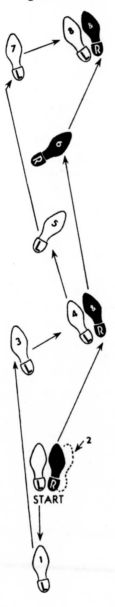

FIRST COMBINATION

Man's Part

COUNT		TIME
1	Cortez bwd L....	S
2	Fwd R.........	S
3-&	Fwd L—swd R..	Q-Q
4	Draw L to R, no weight on L....	S

Repeat from 1st count as desired, or combine with:

5	Swd (or diagonally fwd) L....	S
6	Cross R between self and partner	S
7-&	Fwd L—swd R...	Q-Q
8	Draw L to R, no weight on L...	S

Repeat from 5th count as desired, or combine with first 4 counts.

Figure 35

FIRST COMBINATION

Lady's Part

COUNT		TIME
1	Cortez fwd R....	S
2	Bwd L.........	S
3-&	Bwd R—swd L..	Q-Q
4	Draw R to L, no weight on R...	S

Repeat from 1st count as desired, or combine with:

5	Swd (or diagonally bwd) R...	S
6	Cross L between self and partner	S
7-&	Bwd R—swd L..	Q-Q
8	Draw R to L, no weight on R...	S

Repeat from 5th count as desired, or combine with first 4 counts.

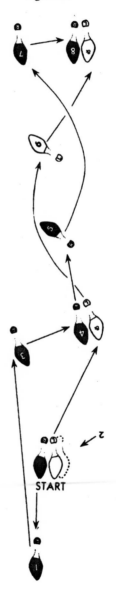

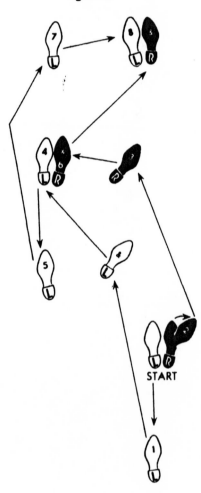

Figure 36

SECOND COMBINATION

Man's Part

COUNT		TIME
1	Cortez bwd L....	S
2-&	Fwd R—swd L...	Q-Q
3	Cross R between self and partner	S
4-&	Swd-close L-R...	Q-Q
5	Cortez bwd L....	S
6	Fwd R.........	S
7-&	Fwd L—swd R..	Q-Q
8	Draw L to R, no weight on L...	S

Repeat as desired from 1st count.

Figure 37

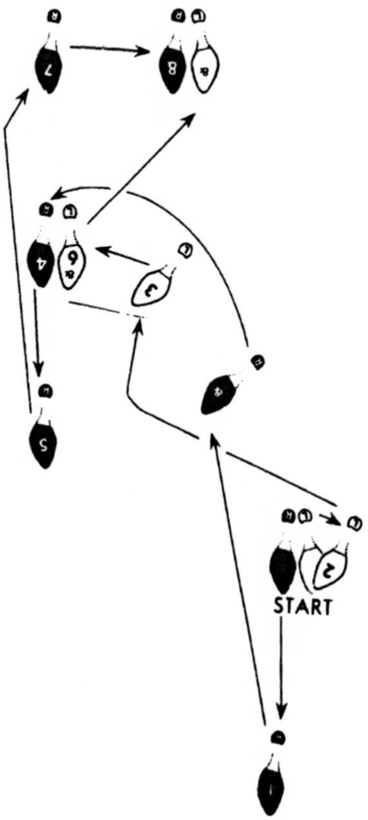

SECOND COMBINATION

Lady's Part

COUNT		TIME
1	Cortez fwd R	S
2-&	Bwd L—swd R ..	Q-Q
3	Cross L between self and partner	S
4-&	Swd-close R-L...	Q-Q
5	Cortez fwd R	S
6	Bwd L..........	S
7-&	Bwd R—swd L ..	Q-Q
8	Draw R to L, no weight on R ...	S

Repeat as desired from 1st count.

Figure 38

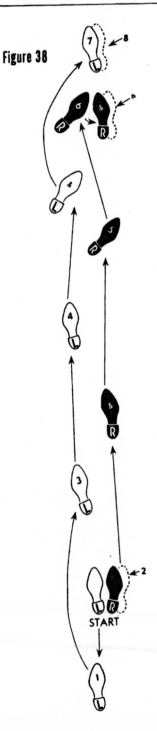

THIRD COMBINATION

Man's Part

COUNT		TIME
1	Cortez bwd L....	S
2	Fwd R.........	S
3-&	Fwd L-R.......	Q-Q
4	Fwd L..........	S
5-&	Fwd R—swd L..	Q-Q
6	Cross R between self and partner	S
7-&	Rock fwd L—bwd R............	Q-Q
8-&	Rock fwd L—bwd R............	Q-Q

Repeat as desired from 1st count.

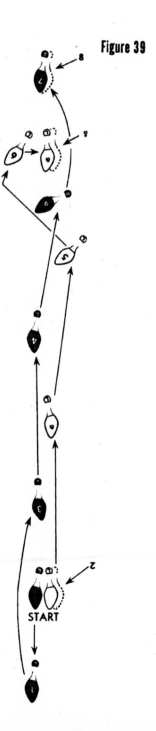

Figure 39

THIRD COMBINATION

Lady's Part

COUNT		TIME
1	Cortez fwd R....	S
2	Bwd L..........	S
3-&	Bwd R-L.......	Q-Q
4	Bwd R........	S
5-&	Bwd L—swd R..	Q-Q
6	Cross L between self and partner	S
7-&	Rock bwd R — fwd L.........	Q-Q
8-&	Rock bwd R — fwd L........	Q-Q

Repeat as desired from 1st count.

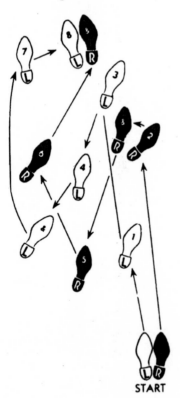

Figure 40

START

FOURTH COMBINATION

Man's Part

Count		Time
1	Swd (or diag fwd to LOD) L....	S
2	Cross R between self and partner	S
3-&	Rock fwd L—bwd R............	Q-Q
4	Bwd L..........	S
5-&	Bwd R—swd L...	Q-Q
6	Cross R between self and partner	S
7-&	Fwd L—swd R ..	Q-Q
8	Draw L to R, no weight on L....	S

Repeat as desired from 1st count.

FOURTH COMBINATION

Lady's Part

Figure 41

COUNT		TIME
1	Swd (or diag bwd to LOD) R	S
2	Cross L between self and partner	S
3-&	Rock bwd R — fwd L	Q-Q
4	Fwd R	S
5-&	Fwd L—swd R . .	Q-Q
6	Cross L between self and partner	S
7-&	Bwd R—swd L . .	Q-Q
8	Draw R to L, no weight on R . . .	S

Repeat as desired from 1st count.

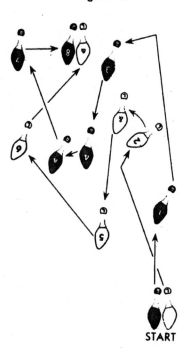

START

The Mambo

THE MAMBO—the latest and the most fascinating addition to the American dance scene—is a syncopated adaptation of the Cuban Bolero and Rumba. In its original form, Mambo is wild, free, and expressive, spiced with the jungle-like rhythm of primitive rituals and folk dance movements. At least some of the original characteristics are retained by Mambo addicts.

Removed from its original habitat, Mambo at once takes its place with other accepted social dances. This is due largely to those far-sighted members of the dance teaching profession who have succeeded in standardizing a modified form of this thrilling dance. To thousands of people—young and old alike—Mambo offers a tantalizing challenge. Here is a dance which demands a maximum of rhythmic sense and response—especially on the part of the lady. Since rhythm and response can be developed, everyone can try the Mambo.

BASIC RHYTHM AND PATTERN

Surprising as it may seem to the uninitiated, Mambo is based on a rhythmic sequence consisting of but six foot movements to two measures (8 beats) of music. It sounds easy and it really is. Once the rhythmic motion has been accomplished, it becomes comparatively easy to change the step pattern to include breaks, commandos, and other standard patterns. It is interesting to note that all the varied positions are used in Mambo: closed position (C-Pos), open break position (OB-Pos), challenge position (CH-Pos) and open position (O-Pos). (*See* Terms and Abbreviations, pp. 1-2.)

Remember that the feet are never brought to the closed position in what is termed the basic step; rather, they are consistently in either a *forward*, *backward*, or *sideward* open position. Also, on the movement Press R bwd, the heel must not be lowered to the floor. (*See* Terms and Abbreviations, pp. 1-2.) On this same step the knee may be slightly bent as the ball of foot receives the weight, but it must not bend after the transfer of weight.

First Half

			DANCE MOVEMENT	
MEAS-URE	TIME	DANCE COUNT	Man's Part	Lady's Part
1	S	4–1	Bwd L	Fwd R
	Q	2	Press R bwd	Press L fwd
	Q	3	SIP L	SIP R

Second Half

2	S	4–1	Fwd R	Bwd L
	Q	2	Press L fwd	Press R bwd
	Q	3	SIP R	SIP L

The first step in each half is counted 4–1. This indicates the last and first beats, respectively, of two succeeding measures of music. In execution, the first step in each half is anticipated; that is, it is started on the last beat of a preceeding measure and held through the first beat of the following measure. With each increase in tempo there is,

among Mambo fans, a tendency to complete the anticipated step closer and closer to the first beat. This sets up
a distinctive rhythm which characterizes Mambo. The
same step pattern, danced within the framework of each
succeeding measure (1-2, 3, 4, 1-2, 3, 4) somehow fails
to meet head-on the challenge hurled by well-regulated
Mambo music.

A close study of the foregoing will acquaint the student
of Mambo with one of its chief characteristics: the constant repetition of the basic rhythmic sequence. Everything else the dancer does can change—step pattern, body
position, etc.—but the rhythmic sequence must never vary
from what a beginner in Mambo might be tempted to refer
to as "monotonous repetition."

Man's Part	TIME	DANCE COUNT	Lady's Part
L	S	4-1	R
R	Q	2	L
L	Q	3	R
R	S	4-1	L
L	Q	3	R
R	Q	3	L

Diligent practice may be required before the movement
becomes automatic and variations follow one another in
perfect timing. A common fault is to execute two slow
steps in succession at any given point in the pattern.
This destroys the basic rhythm and should be corrected
immediately.

As early as possible, an attempt should be made to make
a left turn while doing the basic step. The man can do
this by keeping his glance toward the left and by bearing
in that direction.

Although the Mambo is a constant repetition of the basic *slow-quick-quick* rhythmic pattern, the dancer is urged to take liberties with the step pattern, always keeping in mind that strict adherence to the framework of the rhythm is essential to a correct interpretation.

VARIATIONS IN STEP PATTERN

To change the step pattern merely change the direction of a lead step (4–1); for example, on completion of the "preparation" (first half of the basic step), step *sideward* on 4–1. This develops the pattern which is referred to as the "Cuban (or Open) Break."

The Cuban (or Open) Break

TIME	DANCE COUNT	Man's Part	Lady's Part	POSITION
		Preparation		
S	4–1	Bwd L	Fwd R	C-Pos
Q	2	Press R bwd	Press L fwd	C-Pos
Q	3	SIP	SIP R	C-Pos
		Break		
S	4–1	Swd R	Swd L	OB-Pos
Q	2	Press L bwd	Press R bwd	OB-Pos
Q	3	SIP R	SIP L	OB-Pos

At the beginning of the break, the man releases his hold on the lady with his right hand, so that both may step *backward* and away from each other on 2.

Turnabout and Break

The Turnabout is a movement, consisting of three steps each for the man and the lady, in which a complete but extremely tight circle is made. He circles to his left on L–R–L, and simultaneously she circles to her right on R–L–R. They face each other at the start and at the finish, and the circle described by the movement should be narrow enough in diameter to enable them to remain in close proximity. The challenge position (CH-Pos) is used for this movement, with open break position (OB-Pos) being used on the break.

Turnabout

Man's Part		TIME	DANCE COUNT	Lady's Part	
L	Make tight	S	4–1	R	Make tight
R	circle to	Q	2	L	circle to
L	left	Q	3	R	right

Break

	TIME	DANCE COUNT		
Swd R	S	4–1	Swd L
Press L bwd	Q	2	Press R bwd
SIP R	Q	3	SIP L

A sharp turn on his L on 4–1, and a pedaling movement on the ball of R to lend impetus to the turn on 2 will help the man to complete the circle within a tight radius. The lady turns sharply to her right on 4–1 and follows with a pedal-like movement on the ball of her L on 2.

It is possible to vary the above by using the challenge position throughout the entire movement.

The Commandos

In the foregoing the *closing* step (feet together) has not been used. A somewhat different expression of movement can be realized by *closing* the feet on the lead step (4–1), rather than stepping *fwd*, *bwd*, or *swd* on this beat.

Either of the three positions, C-Pos, OB-Pos, CH-Pos, can be used when doing the Commandos. Assume that a basic step has been completed, then:

Man's Part	TIME	DANCE COUNT	Lady's Part
Right Side Commando			Left Side Commando
Close L	S	4–1	Close R
Press R swd	Q	2	Press L swd
SIP L	Q	3	SIP R
Left Side Commando			Right Side Commando
Close R	S	4–1	Close L
Press L swd	Q	2	Press R swd
SIP R	Q	3	SIP L
Right Back Commando			Left Fwd Commando
Close L	S	4–1	Close R
Press R bwd	Q	2	Press L fwd
SIP L	Q	3	SIP R
Left Fwd Commando			Right Back Commando
Close R	S	4–1	Close L
Press L fwd	Q	2	Press R bwd
SIP R	Q	3	SIP L

Right Fwd Commando: on count 2 Press R fwd.
Left Bwd Commando: on count 2 Press L bwd.

TRIPLE MAMBO

The term "triple" indicates an increase in the number of steps to be taken within the framework of the measure. Instead of six steps, a total of ten steps is possible in the basic two measure Mambo phrase.

Basic Movement

Rather than actual steps, the triple movement is basically a rhythmic reaction; hence a person with slow rhythmic response will not find it easy at first.

The symbol "&" (expressed *and*) is used to count the impulse which occurs between the indicated beats of music (4 & 1). This, in turn, sets up the triple movement resulting in not one, but three steps in exactly the same musical space of time ordinarily devoted to one step.

Man's Part	Time	Dance Count	Lady's Part
Triple Bwd			**Triple Fwd**
L) bwd	S	4	R) fwd
R } SIP	l	&	L } SIP
L) SIP	o	1	R) SIP
	w		
R Press bwd	Q	2	L Press fwd
L SIP	Q	3	R SIP
Triple Fwd			**Triple Bwd**
R) fwd	S	4	L) bwd
L } SIP	l	&	R } SIP
R) SIP	o	1	L) SIP
	w		
L Press fwd	Q	2	R Press bwd
R SIP	Q	3	L SIP

Employing the Triple

Once the technique of the triple has been perfected, it can be superimposed on all Mambo step patterns. The lead step (4–1) is now more than just a *forward* and *backward* movement; it has become an instant of impulsive reaction which has helped to raise Mambo to its present pinnacle of fame and popularity.

The triple movement is basic, and it can be injected wherever the count 4–1 occurs, by changing the count to 4 & 1. Keep in mind that the additional movement should be thought of in terms of an *impulsive reaction* rather than steps. Also remember that injecting the triple in no way changes the musical phrasing; its length remains exactly the same.

Applied to the Commandos, this is the triple effect:

Man's Part	TIME	DANCE COUNT	Lady's Part
L close—R-L SIP	S	4 & 1	R close—L-R SIP
R Press swd (bwd)	Q	2	L Press swd (fwd)
L SIP	Q	3	R SIP
R close—L-R SIP	S	4 & 1	L close—R-L SIP
L Press swd (fwd)	Q	2	R Press swd (bwd)
R SIP	Q	3	L SIP

As indicated, the Commandos can be varied by changing the direction on count 2.

COMBINING THE STEP PATTERNS

The ability to progress from one step pattern to another increases the enjoyment to be derived from Mambo or any other dance. The suggested sequence of the step patterns described here is just one of the dozens used to interpret this new and fascinating rhythm.

Man's Part	DANCE COUNT	Lady's Part
1. Basic Step	4–1, 2, 3, 4–1, 2, 3	Same
2. Cuban Break	4–1, 2, 3, 4–1, 2, 3	Same
3. Turnabout & Break	4–1, 2, 3, 4–1, 2, 3	Same
4. Rt. fwd Commando	4–1, 2, 3	Lt. bwd Commando
Lt. bwd Commando	4–1, 2, 3	Rt. fwd Commando
5. Rt. swd Commando	4–1, 2, 3	Lt. swd Commando
Lt. swd Commando	4–1, 2, 3	Rt. swd Commando
6. Rt. fwd Commando	4–1, 2, 3	Turnabout
Break	4–1, 2, 3	Same

Bear in mind, too, that one does not have to be a contortionist in order to dance and enjoy the Mambo. This dance as usually seen on stage, screen, and television is far removed from its ballroom counterpart.

The Lindy

I T IS nearly thirty years since the Lindy—which seems destined to take its place among the original American folk dances—was first seen in the dance halls of Harlem. Following almost immediately the short-lived Charleston, the Lindy has literally thrived on condemnation and competition. Stripped of ludicrous exhibitionist improvisations, the Lindy is pleasing to the onlooker and a distinct challenge to one's rhythmic ability. As a social dance, it continues to increase in popularity.

Like the Mambo, the Lindy has an individual rhythm, which when learned by the dancer can be injected into various step patterns. Again, like Mambo, the basic rhythm of the Lindy can be "tripled," providing a challenge to rhythmic sense and response.

The rhythm of the Single, or Flat, Lindy consists of four foot movements to one and one-half measure (6 beats) of music in 4/4 time. This results in a timing sequence of *slow-slow-quick-quick*. When the dancer achieves this effect without variation in a succession of step patterns, he has developed an applied rhythmic response—the essence of the Lindy.

The beginner should be concerned chiefly with the Single Lindy, for proficiency in this phase establishes a firm basis for experimentation with the more intricate triple movement.

BASIC RHYTHM AND STEP PATTERN

			DANCE MOVEMENT	
MEAS-URE	TIME	DANCE COUNT	Man's Part	Lady's Part
1	S	1–2	L fwd	R fwd
	S	3–4	R SIP	L SIP
2	Q	5	L Press bwd	R Press bwd
	Q	6	R SIP	L SIP

*Do this three more times within
six measures (24 beats) of music.*

The method of counting (1–2, 3–4, 5, 6) is applied to each repetition of the rhythm and to all variations of the step pattern. Note that the man's R and the lady's L remain in approximately the same position on the floor throughout the pattern; they are raised slightly on each count and lowered in place.

On Press bwd (5), take care not to bend the knee after the transfer of weight and not to lower the heel to the floor. The knee may be slightly bent when the ball of the foot receives the weight (pressure). The resultant effect is a ball change on 5, 6.

When practicing together, the man and the lady stand side-by-side, with his right hand at her waistline, her left hand on his right shoulder. The other hands are clasped. Both dancers move *forward* and *backward* simultaneously.

Too much importance can not be placed upon the rhythmic pattern for it is the basis of the Lindy. The dancer is judged on his or her ability to perform an endless chain movement without once breaking the sequence.

The student will save time and effort if, at first, he con-

fines his practice to the development of the rhythm. To
do this, disregard entirely all step patterns and, for the
present, slightly raise and lower the feet as follows:

Man's Part	TIME	DANCE COUNT	Lady's Part
L	S	1–2	R
R	S	3–4	L
L	Q	5	R
R	Q	6	L
L	S	1–2	R
R	S	3–4	L
L	Q	5	R
R	Q	6	L

When commencing one of the breaks a common fault,
particularly on the lady's part, is to quicken the pace resulting in a series of quick steps on 1–2, 3–4. Regardless
of the direction of a step, or if a turn is indicated on these
counts, strict adherence to the rhythm is essential.

VARIATIONS IN STEP PATTERN

A break in the basic Lindy step pattern consists of doing
something different on 1–2, 3–4. The lady may turn
under her partner's arm; both may separate and do a left
and right turn, respectively, on those two steps. Depend-
ing on the movement effected on 1–2, 3–4, the ball-change
(5, 6) will be done either in the side-by-side position or
with partners facing each other at arm's length.

Always remember to step *backward* on count 5; this is
true for both partners. (If you develop the habit of stepping *forward* on this count, observe the step as danced
correctly and practice it yourself.)

At this point the partners are side-by-side, both facing the center of the room.

The Standard Break

Man's Part	DANCE COUNT	Lady's Part
"A"		**"A"**
L fwd	(S) 1–2	R fwd
R SIP	(S) 3–4	L SIP
L–R B-Ch	(Q–Q) 5, 6	R–L B-Ch
"B"		**"B"**
Repeat above; raise Lt arm	(S) 1–2	R fwd, turn Rt to LOD
to form arch with lady's	(S) 3–4	L bwd toward center
Rt arm.	(Q–Q) 5, 6	R–L B-Ch, facing man

On the counts 1–2 the lady turns outward to the right, under the arch formed by raising her partner's left and her right hand. On the ball-change (5, 6), she must step *backward* towards the center of the room on 5 and *forward* towards her partner on 6. At this point the partners are facing each other joining his left and her right hands at arm's length, with the man facing center and the lady facing the wall.

Here the partners change places; after the move the man is facing the wall and the lady is facing center.

Man's Part	Dance Count	Lady's Part
"C"		"C"
L swd to center	(S) 1–2	R swd to wall, turn Lt
R bwd to center	(S) 3–4	L bwd to wall
L–R B-Ch	(Q–Q) 5, 6	R–L B-Ch

Man: on 1–2 face LOD in order to step *sideward* to center on L; on 3–4 continue to bear Rt until facing wall in order to step *backward* to center on R.

Lady: face wall to start, turn back to partner (to face LOD) and on 1–2 step *sideward* to wall; on 3–4 continue to move *backward* toward wall, and face partner on the step (L bwd).

On the ball-change (5, 6) partners have completely reversed their positions, are again facing each other, and joining his Lt and her Rt hands at arms length.

Variation: release hand clasp (man's Lt, lady's Rt) on 1–2, 3–4 when breaks are indicated on these counts ("B" and "C").

Recovering From Break

Return to the starting position ("A") in the following manner:

Man's Part	DANCE COUNT	Lady's Part
"D"		"D"
L diag fwd	(S) 1–2	R diag fwd
R swd	(S) 3–4	L swd
L–R B-Ch	(Q–Q) 5, 6	R–L B-Ch

On counts 1–2 partners step toward each other, turning slightly toward the clasped hands to resume the side-by-side position. On completion of the step pattern the partners are again facing the center of the room, ready to repeat from the starting position, "A."

TRIPLE LINDY

The term "triple" has the same basic meaning for both the Mambo and the Lindy. It indicates the increase possible in the number of steps within the framework of the measure or count. This movement is more a rhythmic reaction on the part of the dancer than an actual step or transfer of weight. The movement sets in motion an impulse which occurs between the musical beats.

Tripling will make possible a total of six steps within the framework of counts 1–2, 3–4. The timing of *slow-slow* is retained and represents the time consumed for the movements indicated. The symbol "&" (expressed *and*) is used to count the impulse which occurs between the beats as follows: 1-&-2, 3-&-4.

Triple Forward

Man's Part	Dance Count	Time	Lady's Part
L ⎱ fwd R ⎰ SIP L ⎰ SIP	1 & 2	S l o w	R ⎱ fwd L ⎰ SIP R ⎰ SIP

Triple Backward

Man's Part	Dance Count	Time	Lady's Part
R ⎱ SIP L ⎰ SIP R ⎰ SIP	3 & 4	S l o w	L ⎱ SIP R ⎰ SIP L ⎰ SIP
L–R B–Ch	5, 6	Q–Q	R–L B–Ch

Some dancers prefer the "triple forward-single backward" movement, which produces still another rhythmic pattern within the same familiar framework.

Man's Part	Dance Count	Time	Lady's Part
Triple fwd L–R–L	1-&-2	S	Triple fwd R–L–R
R SIP	3–4	S	L SIP
L–R B–Ch	5, 6	Q–Q	R–L B–Ch

The triple movement is basic and can be applied to all the various Lindy step patterns. It must be kept in mind, however, that it does not affect the framework of the count or musical phrasing. Remember, too, that the additional movement created by the injection of the triple should be considered as an *impulsive reaction* rather than an extra step.

Upon application of the triple to either 1–2 or 3–4 when a right or left turn is indicated, the dancer will find himself (and rightly so) doing a version of "step-close-step" within the framework of the count. This will be caused by the momentum set up at the start of the turn.

Once the triple has been accomplished, it will add immeasurable enjoyment to the dance.

CPSIA information can be obtained at www.ICGtesting.com
Printed in the USA
LVOW07s1534170216

475522LV00002B/306/P

9 781445 509624